I0793447

Simultaneous Revolutions

Poems

Marcus Colasurdo and G.H. Mosson

PMPRESS

PM PRESS PAMPHLET SERIES

0001: BECOMING THE MEDIA: A CRITICAL HISTORY OF CLAMOR MAGAZINE
By Jen Angel

0002: DARING TO STRUGGLE, FAILING TO WIN: THE RED ARMY FACTION'S 1977 CAMPAIGN OF DESPERATION
By J. Smith and André Moncourt

0003: MOVE INTO THE LIGHT: POSTSCRIPT TO A TURBULENT 2007
By the Turbulence Collective

0004: THE PRISON-INDUSTRIAL COMPLEX AND THE GLOBAL ECONOMY
By Eve Goldberg and Linda Evans

0005: ABOLISH RESTAURANTS: A WORKER'S CRITIQUE OF THE FOOD SERVICE INDUSTRY
By Prole

0006: SING FOR YOUR SUPPER: A DIY GUIDE TO PLAYING MUSIC, WRITING SONGS, AND BOOKING YOUR OWN GIGS
By David Rovics

0007: PRISON ROUND TRIP
By Klaus Viehmann

0008: SELF-DEFENSE FOR RADICALS: A TO Z GUIDE FOR SUBVERSIVE STRUGGLE
By Mickey Z.

0009: SOLIDARITY UNIONISM AT STARBUCKS
By Staughton Lynd and Daniel Gross

0010: COINTELSHOW: A PATRIOT ACT
By L.M. Bogad

0011: ORGANIZING COOLS THE PLANET: TOOLS AND REFLECTIONS TO NAVIGATE THE CLIMATE CRISIS
By Hilary Moore and Joshua Kahn Russell

0012: "VENCEREMOS": VÍCTOR JARA AND THE NEW CHILEAN SONG MOVEMENT
By Gabriel San Román

0013: ON COMMUNITY CIVIL DISOBEDIENCE IN THE NAME OF SUSTAINABILITY: THE COMMUNITY RIGHTS MOVEMENT IN THE UNITED STATES
By the Community Environmental Legal Defense Fund with an introduction by Thomas Linzey

0014: THAT PRECIOUS STRAND OF JEWISHNESS THAT CHALLENGES AUTHORITY
By Leon Rosselson

0015: DIVIDE AND CONQUER OR DIVIDE AND SUBDIVIDE? HOW NOT TO REFIGHT THE FIRST INTERNATIONAL
By Mark Leier

0016: HEART X-RAYS: A MODERN EPIC POEM
By Marcus Colasurdo and G.H. Mosson

0017: THE YOUNG C.L.R. JAMES: A GRAPHIC NOVELETTE
By Milton Knight * Edited by Paul Buhle and Lawrence Ware

0018: EVENTS AND VICTIMS
By Bartolomeo Vanzetti * Edited by Jon Curley

0019 SIMULTANEOUS REVOLUTIONS: POEMS
By Marcus Colasurdo and G.H. Mosson

PM Press Pamphlet Series No. 0019
Simultaneous Revolutions: Poems
Marcus Colasurdo and G.H. Mosson

ISBN: 978-1-62963-867-6

PM Press
PO Box 23912
Oakland, CA 94623
www.pmpress.org

Second printing. Printed in the UK by Calverts.coop, on recycled paper and vegetable inks.

Simultaneous Revolutions

Contents

I. IF

II. RUMOR

III. FLAGS

1.
IF

Thinking Apart

YOU follow me into the *CONVENIENCE* store,
warehouse rave, bathroom *STALL,* knickknack shop,
down the garbage *CHUTE* of longing
far from those i've *ABANDONED*
because they spoke *GOBBLEDYGOOK* to me
(where even i can't *SEE*) until i suffer
delightfully into some NEW love's arms
to find myself *DANCING*, but
the record has *REPEATED* enough.

I need to *DISCARD* logos and icons
of the cool, dressed-up landscape and HUM what's crude
maybe ethereal *UP*
above the dark *FREE*
as air *ABOUT* us like
loafing in *CHILD*hood's favorite chair
rescued from memory's *JUMBLED* attic
so (not another "you") but all our *TRUEST* names
can be *TOUCHED* through ONE another.

Enter Through *If*

Let's inhabit this music, alone
and not alone, dancing in society's clothes
rearranged from a thrift store, and blur
through the lustful longing of Grimes
on the stage behind her console of giddy electronica
together with us in an abandoned warehouse.

Our harmonies and disharmonies
cross over walls, customs, labels
in wavelengths. Sense the crack,
squeeze through, become a cloud,
embody shapes, touch my body
gentle as drizzle, never look back.

Third Street Deep Blues

It's the middle of the night
    and you find yourself alone.
Downtown, you haven't slept in a day
    and you're getting drowsy,
nodding under a street sign,
3rd Street, it whispers to you,
and you realize
just how strange things are
when you got nowhere to sleep.

You find yourself watching,
waiting to pounce like
some untamed sullen cat.
You feel a moving around inside
    like a blood bubble
that won't let you hide
the things you've been hiding
since way back when.

You see things,
unbelievable things,
and you believe them.
A little girl outside in the rain
crying abandoned
crying hunger
cradled in the torn-tweed arms
of some ancient man.

Both man and child babble at you
and you understand every sound they make
when you got nowhere to live.
You stumble into some pocked, ragged women
scouring garbage cans for supper.
You give your last quarter to a teenage girl
six months pregnant and filthy
from nights under cardboard
when you got nowhere to live.

The cops start looking ten feet tall,
so you find yourself coughing near old hotels
praying for that one-eyed, stoned innkeeper.
But there's no room at the inn tonight
so you find yourself cursing out loud
worried about how long til dawn,
how long the shoes will last,
how long the rain will fall.

You come to see
what's essential
is what can be sold
when you have nowhere
to live, and it makes you
killing mad, but you find
yourself in pay toilets
            in car seats
            in all-night movie theaters
purchased sick, but still purchased
when you have nowhere.

You watch the skyscrapers
      hoping they'll tumble
      and prove Babylon wrong.
And you watch the taxis
      biting your nails
as long-legged blondes lock arms
      with tuxedos of success
and you know furiously
that you still can think
with nowhere to live.

So you walk pressing your
face against restaurant windows,
counting pennies like they're
thousand dollar bills
and you know how impossibly rich
the rich really are
when you got nowhere.

Every doorway is jammed
with sleepers, some of them kids,
already gone, addict gone,

and you wish
you could sweep them up
to somewhere clean
because sometimes
kindness explodes in you.

But all you can do
is keep
walking.
Rain sizzles
your head
as it falls. You don't
have a phone
and no one
to call.
A piece of dry toast
is a feast to you.
And as you walk to nowhere
and back again
as if some mad joke
is being played on you,
you dream of falling in love.

Clouds

Once, desolation pointed a weapon
  at me: I did not look it in the eye.
I did not pray. Instead, I raised
my head to the sky—
someone I think I knew
  told me to, and to this day I cannot say
who that person was, I only know that a soul
can choose to change their name
just by watching.

Cities of lightest eternity,
like lilies in the most ancient garden,
like oldest ships, their sails painted
by all that meets them, clouds like new continents
forming themselves, of necessary magic.
Clouds of wind giants,
behemoths of ice molecules over long hills.

Hallelujah clouds
of liberated cotton fields
tumbleweed past as if in panhandle Texas,
like the horse that Sitting Bull trusted.
Heaped heated haystack clouds, I watch them,
drunken druid dendrite clouds,
cirrus clouds made of grandfather's whiskers,
isis clouds, shapely white-tressed, heavy of belly,
Houdini clouds throwing capes of mystery across the moon.

Sunrise clouds beckoning with crimson feathers,
sunset clouds of finger paint marrying
colors, clouds like yesterday
remembering tomorrow
when the fingers of my childhood
stretched out to the horizon entire—
I have been one of the nation of clouds.

Do you remember the curious quietude
come that prairie afternoon
gathering in helix

swirling to thunderous funnels
of incandescent dazzle?
I remember now the day
when my name became a hymn.
I remember when the air turned green
and fear gave me my life back.
I remember how the sun
shredded my baggage like shrapnel
and I wept in the arms of a stranger.
I remember now how one single cloud
reached down to kiss my pain
and sailed it away.

Ode to Dolores

Can a woman loosen what's hoped
so our hearts jam out in the open?
Can she sing past what's spoken
in the humdrum until
it's unbroken
so our best intent's
again in motion
like Dolores O'Riordan
of The Cranberries,
and how she shared
her emotions, a pugnacious Aphrodite
from some island hamlet
onto the world stage
until fate reclaimed its minute.
Yes, an emerald dazzler
who strutted and solo'd
to where conscience dares
and took us with her
so our pulses merged
into mirrors and made
a second family.

Not Dancing Now

I was a stripper at private parties got paid in cash
and also cleaned my aunt's house when permitted,
paid taxes on it (*no you didn't*) to support my kids (*what trash*)
until bad things happened (*euphemism is appreciated*)
just like my mother who let me be passed about (*and since?*).
I don't speak to her, but I snatch what I want.
You say I'm not truthful, but I speak in wishes.
You say you won't help me, but my good looks taunt,
though I shy from mirrors and see myself in a friend
when I stay on his couch, unlike those high school kids
who jumped me on the bus. Said I looked like a man.
I walked off in the end. Some people can't understand.
And you— can't hear. Echoes block you out.
In rooms, shadows pass. A male voice hisses.
"Hate me, dirty thing." Not real, no doubt.
They just whisper stuff my secrets get.
Haven't seen my kids these last few years
but luv them, just been broke.
Worked last where? Read this stare.
I'll sign your sheet, but I'm no reader.
Sob my story (*your turn*)
to crash at your shelter?
If that's the deal, I'm all in.
Babe, I'm good,
except for the holes.
The knocks hurt.
Help me mend.

Love & Garbage

Drag-racing taxis burst through garbage when we met
where buildings encrusted with ninety years of soot
stood like patient black spiders
yet all of us so impatient
those afternoons at work to get back to
dark clubs with unknown loves
wearing garbage bags as dresses or kilts,
did it matter our gender when our lives were desire?

Next to that blown-up *Sex*
Pistols poster from when they blew through Rose-
land, how you leaned
against the wall, and how I forgot
about tagging graffiti
to whisper, for the first time, "only you"
while waiting
below the CBGB awning
and you purred, "You too."

Our cramped apartment four years later
with a picture of us above my home-office desk
as I'm out on the street picking oranges
for Sunday breakfast, because for us
'no one else is out there,' but
I get pushed. You—above—
in the window—see it.
I wave. I'm OK, and notice how
the shover, almost gone, turns and glares.

I wake up on Monday to your face hovering
above mine badly awake. Are you crying?
I can't quite tell, but I ask, which is why
we are truly friends. Can I unlock myself
and implant you inside, and myself in you?
There is no answer but the question is everything.
We live the question, make love to it.

Sherwood Gardens

Baltimore, Md.

It's not that you go looking for it
in the early May afternoon
with flowers that draw you,
graceful curves of the yellow tulips,
anticipation of azaleas about to burst,
quiet shelter of dogwood blooms,
restfulness that brought you
to your sunny slow-walk
through generous oxygen
among many others lying
down, playing catch, nuzzling
lazy conversations, plus a few,
like you, who saunter, eyes
making love to colors, peaked
ears and perked nostrils, plus
some in turbans,
some in dreads,
some in diapers,
some in skirts,
some in blue jeans,
some in work boots.
No, it's not that you go looking for it, exactly,
but here it is, spacious enough
to allow that one crucial step forward,
pungent enough to let you forget
childhood's first sour lessons:
beware of public smiles,
always run from strangers.
Yet flowers arrive with food for the eyes
and bees tease what's obvious and free
while the breeze interweaves
parades of history into a fade.

II. RUMOR

Construction Site

History
Don't erase
Let's face
TIME
Not a game
To shape life
Into rhyme
MINE
The craft, where'd it go
In the flow
Do you know?

Replace
The chase
With the heart
LET'S GO!
Here I am
Just a man
But a man
DEMAND
Hear my tale
The female
Human
RESPECT
The work of intent
lights the mirror
of the day
so withstand the replay
build forward
don't fade—

Can't hide
from the vision
in the kitchen
as you listen.

Brother lost
in the frost,
here's a coat,
I hear now.

Blues for Allen Ginsberg

Of oldest human wars,
the most intimate is silence,
you broke that mold, didn't you?

As degree-holders, like soldiers,
guard their properties of roses
and statistics command the common good
for a common man—no kicks here, let's beat it.

You stole art from the heart's butcher shop,
howled prayer from a Berkeley backyard
to set words ablaze.
What faded?

Jazzed by a sunflower in a junkyard above
San Francisco Bay, you got wasted
and proclaimed. America moved on
with industrial charm.

Among the push and pull, could you guess
later in knit tie and corduroy jacket in Manhattan,
you'd chant *Holy Holy Holy* from a trash can?

Your oracular bits got junked with Tuesday's
recycling, carted off by everyone's favorite bookie,
that always-dapper building superintendent.

Merry-bearded preacher by the party's bonfire,
you left us more than one candle by which to sing
as clever inventors unreel new machines
(without and within). So what! I'm not running.

Dylan at the Lowlands Cafe

I.
I ask him what he wants.
He says, *What about you?*
Well, that's not my game here.
He says, *Too bad that's true.*

Hey, I work for tips buddy.
Don't we all.
Think it over yet?
He says, *Long ago.*

Listen kid, he leans across
with his fork in the air,
when rolled this far, you arrive
in hindsight. I've been here.

I glance around the diner:
Coffee's on the cool.
Some dude drops three on the table.
The busboy chats up my girl,

Evelyn, early for her shift,
leaning on the counter
by the cakes, as if I'm missed,
or maybe it doesn't matter.

Some jobber eyes that tip
as the rig crew mobs the door.
I might help him join his pals, so
one second, I toss off, toward

this kidder by the window
with a beard like a randy old goat
tattered and what did you say?
He says: *two eggs, bacon, rye toast.*

II.
Old songs, the true, do-or-don't songs, the blues,
take the highway, or the low road, take my way, but with your load,

get young before you get old, get old before you get dumb,
sparkle before sold, feel priceless before worthless,
let's do campfire songs at dawn, wake-up jams at midnight,
belt out ballads in some small town where
the church was bought by the discount chain,
yet I got candlelight; against industrial
production of meaning, let's hum backward
to the flesh-and-blood rodeo, swell
the backyard barbeque chorus against
sundown on the union, find a lounge
to hang with the party crowd
under a statute of Orpheus;
let's shimmy past advertisements
wearing Chuck Berry's white stage shoes
and whistle our ears shut to the musak
from the donkey's theme park
where preachers say religion
is on the side of free candy
for adults convinced no one loves them.
Let's wear sunglasses against talkative
blindness, refuse cookie-cutter questions,
yet tangled up in the road's magic, bust out
into the good news
of the right mood
with a new verse
from some lost tune
in a fresh style
cut loose.

III.

Off to the next town, no
time for plaques or banquets,
name on a billboard, life turned to wind.

Shake off the road burn
because the beat goes on
into dirty blues,

tenement gospel,
pickup-truck folk,
whirligig guitar solos,

rock-and-roll blast-outs,
meandering harmonica,
a dive into the mirror

where I too tangoed
with a few sweethearts
where rhythm operates and cures;

so "Travel Lite Pal,"
"Dance With The Brightest Eyes Around,"
for "At Dawn, We're Gone."

IV.
Hey Jimmy, where did
that old feller go,
I asked my manager,
the thing he's good for,

being a fat lookout.
That goat in Booth Four,
I said, did he skip the bill
and hop out the door?

Jimmy said, look at this
Hundred Dollar Smacker
with a scribbled note on it:
"Use it well, Waiter."

Magnificent Rumor

The first thing I hear with my good ear:
The Clash's haywire guitar
and a tin can kicked
against the dole office door
splattered like cheap food.
A crowd is calling
for unheard-of chords,
snarldodging the clampdown.
A single brick spiders the lettered
display window of a chain store
and splinters tomorrow's headlines.
Hear it? The old Empire is wearing
thin its diction, and the Union Jack's
been defrocked back to some pirate symbol.
The tumult trembles the bank vault
creaking it open: empty.
General strike rock-and-roll!
Somewhere on stage
a singer mohawks the blues
and soon enough youthful boots
Bo Diddley the roof
of the House of Lords
while tear gas gangs up
on the mouths of the coal mines.
Do ya hear it?

Listen, if your minutes
belong to my hours
we'll meet near the street
where all that graffiti
wonderlands the wounded.
Hear it?
I do.
I think I hear you
      coming nearer
            to me.

The Tyrant

Your ignorance my strategy,
your greed my fuel,
your yes my boon,
your no, my jack-in-the-box.

Your protests cannot find me.
I'm untouched by pleas.
That brittle god of yours cannot lasso me.
He's just you trying to forgive yourself.

Keep looking I'm not ducking,
keep pretending I'm not playing,
keep forgiving I'm not giving back,
keeping cheating I'll buy.

What to make of my disappearances
when you approach? How quick I seem
someone else, while you rush to become
what you're not with my stuff.

Sorry my tools were faulty.
You paid heavily, didn't you?
So sad to get off track and lose yourself.

Did I foul the waters of the critics?
Who knows. A mirror, I'm told
is just something made of sand.

Liberté Haikus

Standing Rock, tear-gassed,
now come cuffs from oil man's cops,
we hold sacred ground.

We kneel, Saint Louis,
and pray for the gunned-down child.
When we rise, justice.

To a homeless soul
this Vermont winter, the boon
of one hot shower.

How many more wounds
will the earth endure before
she withdraws balance?

While counting your friends
on the screen of a machine,
who kisses your tears?

Like branches, to stretch
with respect toward those not met
seeds a canopy.

Soulphone Ringing

I.
I went down with my soulphone to see
what might amaze me in the big city
from my parents' home
and got a call selling a 99-cent song
about freedom, but I took another call.
The wheel spun of course
and I don't have that long
to tell this, but last night after
dinner my kids asked, "Where's
the Cherry Garcia, Dad,"
and I shrugged because
who could mutter, I'm short,
or bark about the crap luck
playing poker last Saturday
at Fat Jack's Funk Shack,
another mistake I'm reliving
even if my best friend Ralph
cheered me on, and steered
me wrong to bluff
at the worst turn
against a crown flush.
What a bust. Why's
quick risk a must? Can't
keep chasing that hole.
Plus, Janet doesn't know yet
how the rent got sucked
up by a bum card
though the overtime list
at the shop's still got a slot.
Get that sewn up. Pray
for courage to tell her
from my knees, and plant
myself deeper into her heart,
before she screams, *Get Out*,
because we are not too far
from our teenage dreams
despite how different it
all seems. Well, with no one

awake but the mirror, I'm
gonna sing about reform.

II.
Headed down the wounded highway
like a nurse on the same road,
don't know what the banners say today,
but sense the ill from the good.

III.
"Hey Billy, got yer parcel ! Good changes
in yr life man, thanks for the news and banana bread.
Quit smoking, quit gambling, and back in the gym, I guess
the next step's religion. LOL! "And I wept in the arms of a stranger,"
as you wrote—haven't we all, brother.
Well, I'm still livin' well in Missoula
& don't think I'll be working elections
anymore. Old bones can't do 80-hour weeks
despite the dream of some other world
a-swirl around my head—as if I dwelled
in one of those books glancing from wooden
shelves built in high school, and still got 'em.
Woodworking has blossomed into a business
and not a bad one. Solid in fact as it keeps
me here and grounded. Plus, I garden
and Sam, remember her? We're living
together now, our first year. I've decided
to let the next generation change the world—
not that you didn't laugh back then to harangues
from the backyard soapbox, in Dad's yard
of course. But don't think I haven't
thought some of the answers
right through to the questions.
What IS revolutionary . . . what action,
work is FUNDAMENTALLY different from the old . . .
Thinking about soil . . . planting . . . upheaval . . .
how the turning of the soil, come spring,
reveals uses of the dead
and yes, how what dies
releases nitrogen which
enriches the earth
as revolution includes evolution

in substance through decomposition,
a creative act yielding
new growth. It keeps us all alive.
What if a mind thought about $$$$$$ that way?
Dreaming a lot this week,
          Much luv bro,
          the Other Bill."

IV.
So come to Fat Jack's Funk Shack,
you have to park and then just walk,
full price if you buy with credit,
half price if you talk.

Lehigh River Gorge

Jim Thorpe, Pa.

The afternoon turns cold as we
are slated to arrive upon a rise
of snow-scented wind
singing through the leavings.
Ghostly hemlocks whisper
among the mossed ruins
of the old stone tanneries
about the clamorous days
a century past, when hides
where taken from rabbit and deer
beneath barren November birches
like these, from beaver and bear,
hides taken and cured, taken
and shipped south, hauled north,
railed west, freighted east
to warm the backs of winter walkers
in the outposts of the blooming,
booming, troubled Republic.

Today, we listen
  and in our walking
we keep close to one another
reaching a right hand
gloved into a left one
and alert to the rush of the flow
below.
        Although
something about this river
makes me want her,
I do not speak a word.

Above, through the glass-cut hiss
of first sleet, a nation is forming
in the darkening sky,
honking and squawking
making itself known.

In the tempo of change
and variable of leadership
moves a migration
over these original hills.
Above us, a stark deep V
    has emerged
      bird after bird
        containing a strength
      of memory
    from before my kind
had a language.

Against the stained eggshell clouds
these geese speak to the river
and even a man in love
with the woman who warms him
must surely discern
he's not chosen
to answer the calls
of this harmonic flight.

III.
FLAGS

Tilling

The earth feels endless, a teacher of depths.
In the sun, working the dirt,
I've come to know
the turning of soil,
how it yields old surprises.
Under my blades,
clods and clumps fly up
brown and web-woven;
stones exchange silent respect;
and a tiny ivory onion
falls asleep in the palm
of the spade.
Worms ooze, uprooted.
An eggshell winks
and small birds slowly draw closer
to my kneeling
as above the sepia clouds
whirl and an odd sort of freshness
blends with my sweat.

Tilling: In short time,
the back grows stronger.
It's that kind of work.
These arms bronze over
hard-glossed by the heat.
As fields I've found
call me further, I dig into
independence, to grow my own food,
into the loamy vernal labor,
and begin to resemble someone
I thought I'd forgotten.

Highway Hymn

When a jumbo jet low
over the thruway
crossed more luminous
than dawn's lingering moon,
I had places to go
and work to knock out
as if some arrow
was pulling me through
the chaos of this ancient orb.
Soon after, a smaller plane
zoomed over in pastel colors,
metallic remake of a bird
impressing we are transformers
as if spun from some prehistoric tongue
to live this dazzle
of replica upon replica
knowing ourselves
only through exhale
of unstoppable phenomena.

Ode to a Mailbox

Mini-behemoth of promised motion,
short, squat, rounded at the top,
stationary caboose car
stamped onto the sidewalk
under a tall oak tree
of my neighborhood;
mute receiver of envelopes,
bills come due, womb
of congratulations, penciled
complaints, condolence cards,
halfway house for urgent epistles
on exodus from nearby addresses,
endangered species some would say,
or just a nostalgic warrior out-
numbered by the electronic horde.

Keeper of secrets, lips zipped tight,
painted blue and white, stumpy beacon
above the snowfall, perhaps
the futurists are right about you, yet
the mailbox still anchors
how I live, as much
as any azalea bush,
speed bump or stop sign,
or children's hopscotch.

Ah mailbox, I will continue
to visit you regardless of the cynics
and their haste, and arrow
my evening stroll your way
for whatever else is said
in capitals of state
and salons of silver,
we've known each other
for these long seasons
and not once
have you betrayed me.

How to Fix?

So what if this tooth was bashed,
so what if the dentist was careless,
and the mess exhausted my cash,
so what if he's left with his business.

Which hand or hello that extends
from website or billboard might help?
What happened to all my friends?
Too busy saving ourselves.

By which sign on the road might I find
what I've lost? Have you seen?
Where to go and how to fix
why I'm lonely. . . .

Chesapeake Summer Music

1. Way out here,
the Chesapeake stretches
as if some long, fat
complicated snake
curves awake from hibernation,
flicking her tongue
as
an
arrow
toward the Atlantic's vast rhythm of breath.
Way out here,
listen:

2. The sweet June breeze
through the hair of the trees
seems the beginning of
some
sunny
symphony—
while down below
the wind so slow
creeps through the heat,
but picking up the roll,
bends back the tall marsh grass,
flattening the thin, fibered stalks,
until the earth here
looks like a moving page
of gypsy lowland sheet music
written in green ink.

3. Across the froggy creek,
a tractor's harrow disc
spins like a shiny LP
clearing a field
as if preparing a dance ground
where in the wake
of its chukka-chukka shake
funnels of dirt arise:
barley brown clumps

of twirling clod
like the native ghosts
of those old
fancy dancers
come alive
with the sun in their eyes:
dusty
fertile
proud.

4. Down at the sound
the work boats waking up
crank the morning
from bob to throb
with engine-eaten diesel
like three lightning power chords.
The watermen are talkin'
the rockfish are runnin'
and the crabs struttin'.

Might as well follow
that old slop of song
and get to dancin'
while the water holds gems.
Might as well move
while there's still
brine in my spine.

5. School's out !
and
the car's ours tonight !
grab a lover
or someone who's game
and fire up that one
long liberty song !
Let 'em hear you all down the Atlantic.
Come dawn, the game's got claws.

Flag (Road Work Ahead)

What would it broadcast, the flag
of the future conceived by your heart?
What cloth would you choose
to make public and plain
the look of your dreams?
Through what language seen
out of blood and brains
would you stitch
the totem of your settlement?
What ceremony would you enact
to beckon the wind come bless
and imbue what you imagined
with the gladdening of breezes?
What symbols,
        what words,
                what colors
would you scroll across
        the first fluttering pages
of your nation's rising soul?
And what if—suddenly!—
no later than sunrise, tomorrow,
the task becomes yours to fulfill?

About the Authors

Marcus Colasurdo is the author of eleven books, including the underground classic novel *Angel City Taxi* and *Heart X-rays* with G.H. Mosson (PM Press, 2018). Over the years, he has worked as a bartender, boom microphone operator, waiter, taxicab driver, factory worker, Job Corps counselor, farmworker, journalist, construction laborer, teacher, and more. His explorations have taken him across the length and breadth of the United States, a significant part of it achieved through the lost art of hitchhiking. As a writer for the page and stage, Mr. Colasurdo also is the founder of Gimme Shelter Productions, a nonprofit organization of artists whose performances benefit homeless shelters, feeding programs, and other worthy causes. More recently, Mr. Colasurdo helped found Soul Kitchens in Baltimore, Maryland, and Hazelton, Pennsylvania, which provide free meals to those who need them with the goal of culinary panache and deep-rooted nourishment for all who come to eat, volunteer, and be present. Mr. Colasurdo hails from the anthracite coal country of Pennsylvania.

G.H. Mosson is the author of four prior books of poetry, including *Family Snapshot as a Poem in Time* (Finishing Line Press, 2019) and *Heart X-rays* with Marcus Colasurdo (PM Press, 2018). His poetry has appeared in *The Hollins Critic*, *The Tampa Review*, *The Cincinnati Review*, *Measure*, and *The Evening Street Review*. From 2003 to 2010, he edited *Poems Against War: A Journal of Poetry and Action*, including the anthology *Poems Against War: Bending Toward Justice* (Wasteland Press, 2010). A writer, father, and lawyer, Mr. Mosson over the years has organized for fair trade, not free trade, and for environmental conservation. As part of this journey, he has taught legal writing and advocacy at the University of Baltimore School of Law; and literature and writing at Johns Hopkins University, among other places. With Mr. Colasurdo, he has performed as part of Gimme Shelter Productions. Mr. Mosson hails from NYC and lives in his second home state of Maryland.

PM Press is an independent, radical publisher of books and media to educate, entertain, and inspire. Founded in 2007 by a small group of people with decades of publishing, media, and organizing experience, PM Press amplifies the voices of radical authors, artists, and activists. Our aim is to deliver bold political ideas and vital stories to all walks of life and arm the dreamers to demand the impossible. We have sold millions of copies of our books, most often one at a time, face to face. We're old enough to know what we're doing and young enough to know what's at stake. Join us to create a better world.

PM Press
PO Box 23912
Oakland CA 94623
510-658-3906
www.pmpress.org

PM Press in Europe
europe@pmpress.org
www.pmpress.org.uk

Friends of PM

These are indisputably momentous times—the financial system is melting down globally and the Empire is stumbling. Now more than ever there is a vital need for radical ideas.

In the many years since its founding—and on a mere shoestring—PM Press has risen to the formidable challenge of publishing and distributing knowledge and entertainment for the struggles ahead. With hundreds of releases to date, we have published an impressive and stimulating array of literature, art, music, politics, and culture. Using every available medium, we've succeeded in connecting those hungry for ideas and information to those putting them into practice.

Friends of PM allows you to directly help impact, amplify, and revitalize the discourse and actions of radical writers, filmmakers, and artists. It provides us with a stable foundation from which we can build upon our early successes and provides a much-needed subsidy for the materials that can't necessarily pay their own way. You can help make that happen—and receive every new title automatically delivered to your door once a month—by joining as a Friend of PM Press. And, we'll throw in a free T-shirt when you sign up.

Here are your options:

- $30 a month: Get all books and pamphlets plus 50% discount on all webstore purchases
- $40 a month: Get all PM Press releases (including CDs and DVDs) plus 50% discount on all webstore purchases
- $100 a month: Superstar—Everything plus PM merchandise, free downloads, and 50% discount on all webstore purchases

For those who can't afford $30 or more a month, we have *Sustainer Rates* at $15, $10, and $5. Sustainers get a free PM Press T-shirt and a 50% discount on all purchases from our website.

Your Visa or Mastercard will be billed once a month, until you tell us to stop. Or until our efforts succeed in bringing the revolution around. Or the financial meltdown of Capital makes plastic redundant. Whichever comes first.

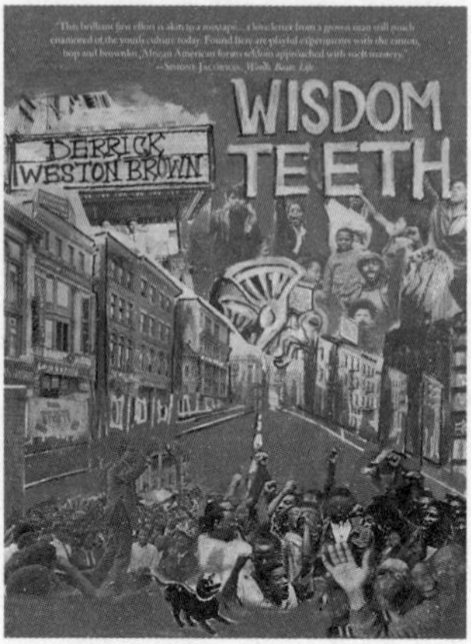

Wisdom Teeth

Derrick Weston Brown

Foreword by Simone Jacobson

ISBN: 978-1-60486-417-5

$14.95

To consider *Wisdom Teeth* is to acknowledge inevitable movement, shift, and sometimes pain. There's change hidden just below the surface and, like it or not, once it breaks, everything has to make room. So goes the aptly titled debut poetry collection from poet and educator Derrick Weston Brown. *Wisdom Teeth* reveals the ongoing internal and external reconstruction of a poet's life and world, as told through a litany of forms and myriad of voices, some the poet's own.

Wisdom Teeth is a questioning work, a redefining of personal relationships, masculinity, race, and history. It's a readjustment of bite, humor, and perspective as Brown channels hip-hop, Toni Morrison, and Snagglepuss to make way for the shudder and eruption of wisdom.

> *"This brilliant first effort is akin to a mixtape, filled with nostalgic hip-hop references—MF Doom, A Tribe Called Quest, and J Dilla, among others—a love letter from a grown man still much enamored of the youth culture today. Found here are playful experiments with the eintou, bop, and brownku, African American forms seldom approached with such mastery."*
>
> —Simone Jacobson, managing editor for *Words. Beats. Life: The Global Journal of Hip-Hop Culture*

Late in the Day

Poems 2010–2014

Ursula K. Le Guin

ISBN: 978-1-62963-122-6

$18.95

Late in the Day, Ursula K. Le Guin's newest collection of poems, seeks meaning in an ever-connected world. In part evocative of Neruda's *Odes to Common Things* and Mary Oliver's poetic guides to the natural world, Le Guin gives voice to objects that may not speak a human language but communicate with us nevertheless through and about the seasonal rhythms of the earth, the minute and the vast, the ordinary and the mythological.

As Le Guin herself states, "science explicates, poetry implicates." Accordingly, this immersive, tender collection implicates us (in the best sense) in a subjectivity of everyday objects and occurrences. Deceptively simple in form, the poems stand as an invitation both to dive deep and to step outside of ourselves and our common narratives. As readers, we emerge refreshed, having peered underneath cultural constructs toward the necessarily mystical and elemental, no matter how late in the day.

The poems are bookended with two short essays, "Deep in Admiration" and "Form, Free Verse, Free Form: Some Thoughts."

> *"She never loses touch with her reverence for the immense what is."*
>
> —Margaret Atwood

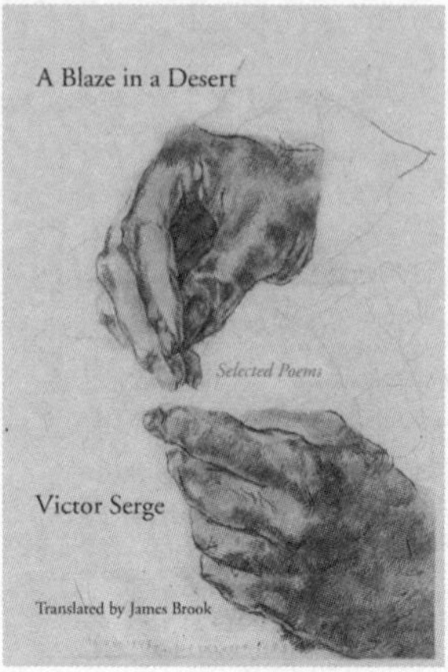

A Blaze in a Desert

Selected Poems

Victor Serge

Edited and translated by James Brook

Afterword by Richard Greeman

ISBN: 978-1-62963-382-4
$16.95

Victor Serge (1890–1947) played many parts, as he recounted in his indelible *Memoirs of a Revolutionary.* The son of anti-czarist exiles in Brussels, Serge was a young anarchist in Paris; a syndicalist rebel in Barcelona; a Bolshevik in Petrograd; a Comintern agent in Central Europe; a comrade of Trotsky's; a friend of writers like Andrei Bely, Boris Pilnyak, and André Breton; a prisoner of Stalin; a dissident Marxist in exile in Mexico . . .

Like Serge's extraordinary novels, *A Blaze in a Desert: Selected Poems* bears witness to decades of revolutionary upheavals in Europe and the advent of totalitarian rule; many of the poems were written during the "immense shipwreck" of Stalin's ascendancy. In poems datelined Petrograd, Orenburg, Paris, Marseille, the Caribbean, and Mexico, Serge composed elegies for the fallen—as well as prospective elegies for the living who, like him, endured prison, exile, and bitter disappointment in the revolutions of the first half of the twentieth century:

Night falls, the boat pulls in,
stop singing.
Exile relights its captive lamps
on the shore of time.

Throughout *A Blaze in a Desert*, Serge draws on the heritage of late- and post-Symbolist writers like Verhaeren, Rictus, Apollinaire, Blok, and Bely—themselves authors of messages of a more general resistance by the human spirit—to express the anguish of the failure of the Russian Revolution and to search out glimmers of hope in the ruins of the Second World War.

A Blaze in a Desert comprises Victor Serge's sole published book of poetry, *Resistance* (1938), his unpublished manuscript *Messages* (1946), and his last poem, "Hands" (1947).

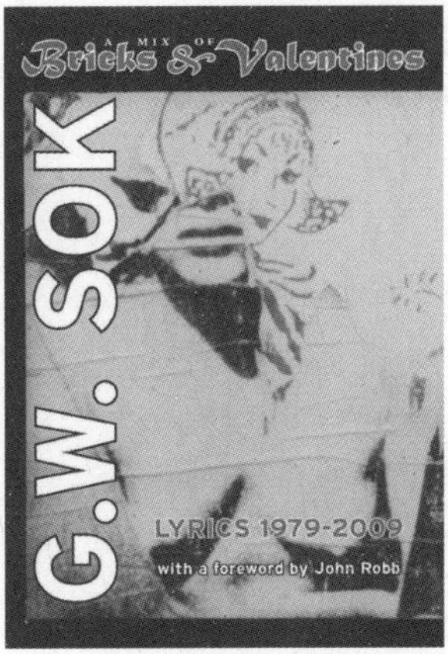

A Mix of Bricks & Valentines

Lyrics 1979–2009

G.W. Sok

Foreword by John Robb

ISBN: 978-1-60486-499-1

$20.00

G.W. Sok co-founded of the internationally acclaimed independent Dutch music group The Ex in 1979. He became the singer and lyricist, more or less by coincidence, since he wrote the occasional poem and nobody else wanted to sing. At the same time he turned himself into a graphic designer of record sleeves, posters, and books. Together with The Ex he was awarded the Dutch Pop Prize of 1991. The band is well known for their energetic live performances, inventive music, and politically outspoken and thought-provoking lyrics. After 1,400 concerts in Holland and abroad, and 25 record albums later, G.W. Sok decided to leave the group at the end of 2008.

A Mix of Bricks & Valentines showcases the lyrics G.W. Sok wrote during his three-decade period of Ex-istence. More than 250 songs of agitprop lyrics, poetry, and rantings are included along with an introduction by the author discussing his development as a writer. A foreword by English journalist, author, and musician John Robb (the Membranes, *Punk: An Oral History* and *Death to Trad Rock*) puts the work of G.W. Sok into perspective.

A Mix of Bricks & Valentines is written with a sharp pen; provocative, creative, and witty, everything punk and art intended to be from the start. And yes, it can be quite loud at times, too.

> *"Lyrically, The Ex is also in a class of its own. This is rebel punk's finest hour."*
> —SF Weekly

Heart X-rays

A Modern Epic Poem

Marcus Colasurdo and G.H. Mosson

ISBN: 978-1-62963-513-2

$5.95

Heart X-rays is a twenty-first-century beat epic poem that ranges across landscapes and voices, with appearances by Banksy, Pussy Riot, hip-hop, the down and out, the up and coming, heartbreak and joybreak, while exploring the mystery we call the human heart.

Now in its second printing, *Heart X-rays* offers poetry that strikes a cord today with non-traditional style and timeless poetic craft.

If indeed poetry can offer an RX, a prescription to the bloody joyful teary-eyed American paradox, it is one that calls forth all the voices that have not yet been heard, that harbors an innocence that reaches into the very heart of our own excellence. A collaborative work between two poets and working-class activists, *Heart X-rays* is a poetic memory of today written in the alphabet of a future.

> *"I think more highly of* Heart X-rays *now in my eighty-fourth year than I thought of Allen Ginsberg's* Howl *when I heard him read it in 1956. Colasurdo and Mosson, in a demonstration of democratic commitment making no distinction as to who wrote which poem, reveal to us the cutting edge, the real news of our society as opposed to the white noise of our society which we call news in our surrender to corporate myth-making."*
>
> —Djelloul Marbrook, *JMWW Journal*